William B Blake

Sweet Fields of Eden

For the Sabbath School

William B Blake

Sweet Fields of Eden
For the Sabbath School

ISBN/EAN: 9783743325142

Manufactured in Europe, USA, Canada, Australia, Japa

Cover: Foto ©Lupo / pixelio.de

Manufactured and distributed by brebook publishing software (www.brebook.com)

William B Blake

Sweet Fields of Eden

MUSIC SCHOOL.

WE TEACH ALL BRANCHES.
PRICES VERY MODERATE.

Write for Our Terms if You are in Anyway Interested in
SCHOOL WORK.

BOARD, ROOM, TUITION AND WASHING ONLY $15.00
PER MONTH.

OPEN FROM SEPTEMBER TO JUNE.

ADDRESS,

J. H. RUEBUSH,

DAYTON, - - - VA.

SWEET FIELDS OF EDEN;

FOR THE

SABBATH SCHOOL.

BY

J. H. TENNEY, ALDINE S. KIEFFER,

WM. B. BLAKE.

RUEBUSH, KIEFFER & CO.,

Music Publishers,

DAYTON, Rockingham Co., Virginia.

1882.

DEDICATION

To the Sabbath School children of America;
  To the friends of Sacred song; and
    To all who wait and watch for the appearing of
OUR LORD AND SAVIOR, JESUS CHRIST,
and for that glorious day when the "wilderness shall blossom as the rose," and when "the land shall be as the garden of Eden before them," this volume, "SWEET FIELDS OF EDEN," is respectfully dedicated.

If anticipations of the great company, who stand in white about the THRONE, and their blest employment, are numerous in this little book, it is because the theme is precious to the writers.

March 10, 1882.

J. H. TENNEY.
A. S. KIEFFER.
W. B. BLAKE.

THE SCALE.

Doe, Ray, Mee, Faw, Sole, Law, See, Doe, Doe, See, Law, Sole, Faw, Mee, Ray, Doe.

Entered, according to Act of Congress, in the year 1882, by
RUEBUSH, KIEFFER & CO.,
in the Office of the Librarian of Congress, at Washington, D. C.

J. M. ARMSTRONG & CO., MUSIC TYPOGRAPHERS, Philadelphia.

BRINGING IN THE SHEAVES. CONCLUDED.

joic-ing, bring-ing in the sheaves. Bringing in the sheaves, Bringing in the
Bringing in the golden sheaves, Bringing in the
sheaves, We shall come re - joic - ing, bring - ing in the sheaves.
gold - en sheaves.

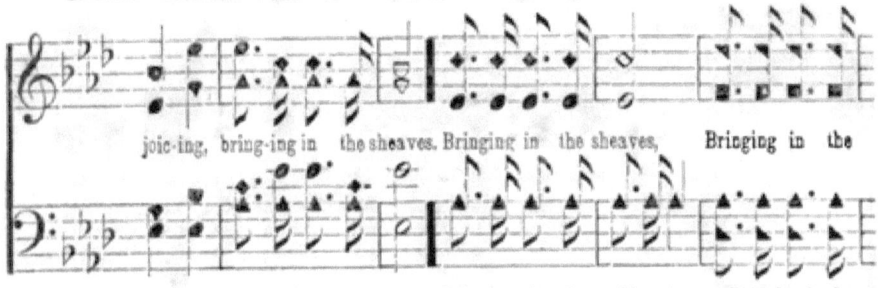

SCHILLER. C. M.

O. J. MILLER.

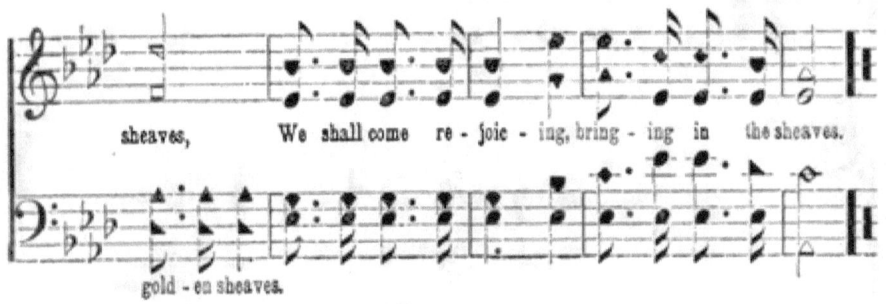

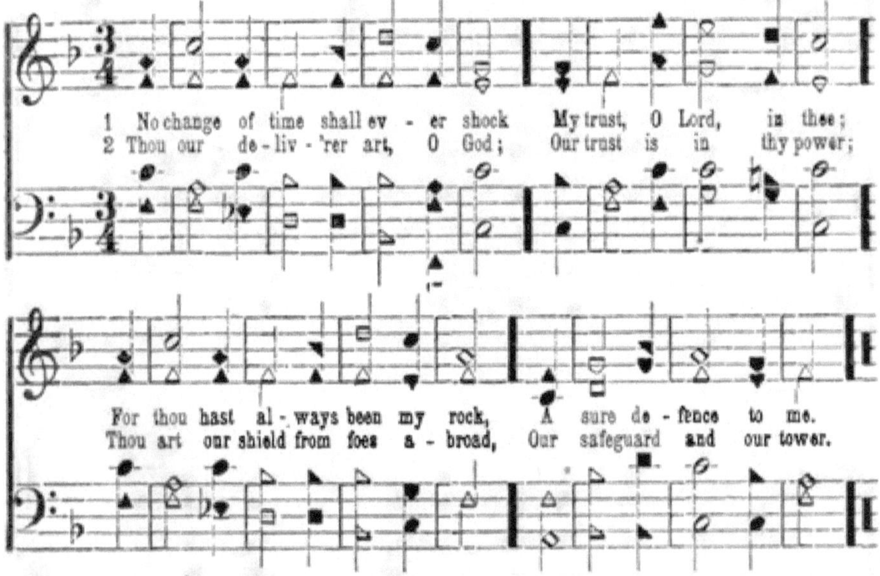

1 No change of time shall ev - er shock My trust, O Lord, in thee;
2 Thou our de - liv - 'rer art, O God; Our trust is in thy power;
For thou hast al - ways been my rock, A sure de - fence to me.
Thou art our shield from foes a - broad, Our safeguard and our tower.

3 To thee will we address our prayer,
To whom all praise we owe;
O, may we, by thy watchful care
Be saved from every foe.

4 Then let Jehovah be adored.
On whom our hopes depend;
For who, except the mighty Lord,
His people can defend?

2 Wildly the storm sweeps us on as it roars,
   We're homeward bound;
  Look! yonder lie the bright heavenly shores,
   We're homeward bound;
  Steady, O pilot! stand firm at the wheel,
  Steady! we soon shall outweather the gale;
  Oh, how we fly 'neath the loud creaking sail,
   We're homeward bound.

3 Into the harbor of heaven we glide,
   We're home at last;
  Softly we drift o'er its bright silver tide,
   We're home at last;
  Glory to God! all our dangers are o'er,
  We stand secure on the glorified shore;
  Glory to God! we will shout evermore,
   We're home at last.

I AM WAITING. CONCLUDED.

jour-ney's al-most o'er, I am wait-ing, yes, I'm wait-ing to go home.

GREENVILLE.

J. J. ROSSEAU.

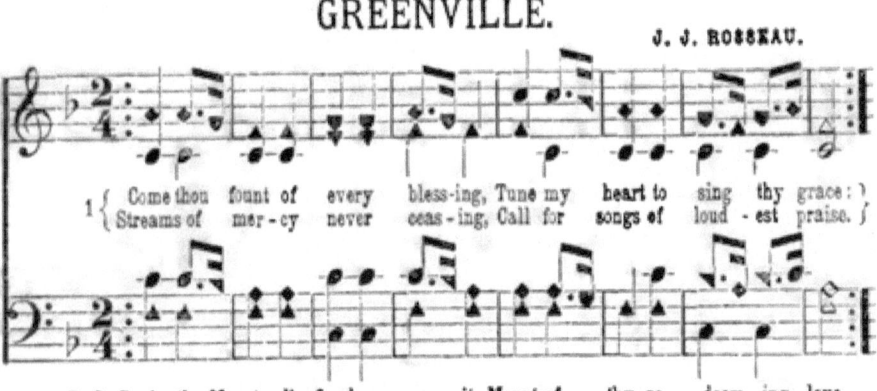

1 { Come thou fount of every bless-ing, Tune my heart to sing thy grace:
    Streams of mer-cy never ceas-ing, Call for songs of loud-est praise. }

D. C. Praise the Mount—I'm fixed up-on it, Mount of thy re-deem-ing love.

Teach me some mel-o-dious son-net, sung by flam-ing tongues a-bove:

2
Here I'll raise mine Ebenezer,
　Hither by thy help I'm come;
And I hope, by thy good pleasure,
　Safely to arrive at home.
Jesus sought me, when a stranger,
　Wand'ring from the fold of God;
He, to rescue me from danger,
　Interposed his precious blood.

3
O! to grace how great a debtor
　Daily I'm constrained to be!
Let thy goodness, like a fetter,
　Bind my wand'ring heart to thee!
Prone to wander, Lord, I feel it:
　Prone to leave the God I love—
Here's my heart, O take and seal it!
　Seal it for thy courts above.

COME TO THE CROSS OF JESUS.

C. M. H. REV. C. M. HOTT.

3 Ye who are hardened and far away,
   Come to the Cross of Jesus.
   Hear him so tenderly plead to-day,
   Come to the Cross of Jesus.
   Though you have slighted his love so long,
   Gone with your heart in the ways of wrong,
   Still he will save with his arm so strong,
   Come to the Cross of Jesus.

4 Why will you die when there yet is room?
   Come to the Cross of Jesus.
   Why will you perish in sight of home?
   Come to the Cross of Jesus.
   What will you do when He comes at last?
   How can you live till his wrath is past!
   Oh, heed this call, it may be the last!
   Come to the Cross of Jesus.

IN THE SHADOW OF HIS WING. CONCLUDED.

LULEMON. 7s.

S. H. SWANK.

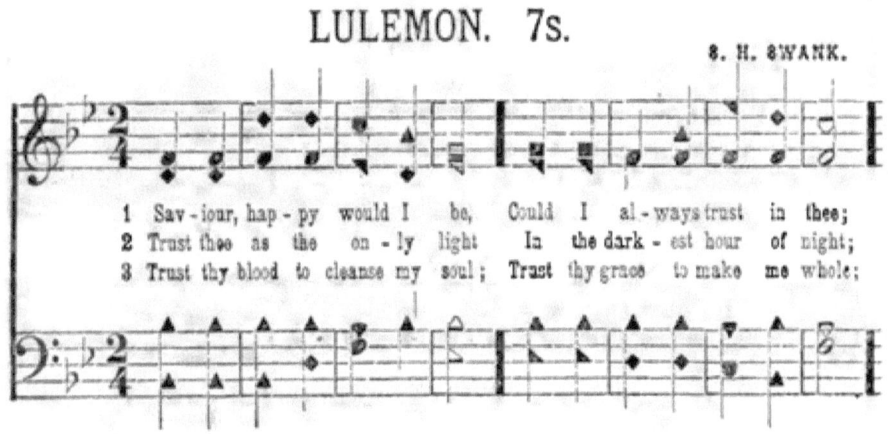

1 Sav-iour, hap-py would I be, Could I al-ways trust in thee;
2 Trust thee as the on-ly light In the dark-est hour of night;
3 Trust thy blood to cleanse my soul; Trust thy grace to make me whole;

Trust thy wis-dom me to guide; Trust thy good-ness to pro-vide.
Trust in sick-ness, trust in health; Trust in pov-er-ty and wealth.
Trust thee liv-ing, dy-ing, too; Trust thee all my jour-ney through.

ONE DAY NEARER HOME.

J. H. TENNEY.

Slowly and gently.

1 O'er the hill the sun is set-ting, And the eve is draw-ing on,
2 "One day near-er," sings the sail-or, As he glides the wa-ters o'er,
3 Worn and wea-ry, oft the pil-grim Hails the set-ting of the sun,
4 Near-er home! yes, one day near-er To our Fa-ther's house on high,

Slow-ly drops the gen-tle twi-light, For an-oth-er day is gone;
While the light is soft-ly dy-ing On his dis-tant na-tive shore;
For the goal is one day near-er, And his jour-ney near-ly done;
To the green fields and the foun-tains Of the land be-yond the sky;

Gone for aye, its race is o-ver, Soon the dark-er shades will come,
Thus the Chris-tian on life's o-cean, As his life-boat cuts the foam,
Thus we feel, when o'er life's des-ert, Heart and san-dal worn we roam,
For the heav'ns grow bright-er o'er us, And the lamps hang in the dome,

Still 'tis sweet to know at e-ven We are one day near-er home.
In the eve-ning cries with rap-ture, "I am one day near-er home."
As the twi-light gath-ers o'er us, We are one day near-er home.
And our tents are pitched still clo-ser, For we're one day near-er home.

THE PURE WATER OF LIFE. CONCLUDED.

LAND IMMORTAL.

THOS. MACKELLAR. FRANCIS A. EVANS.

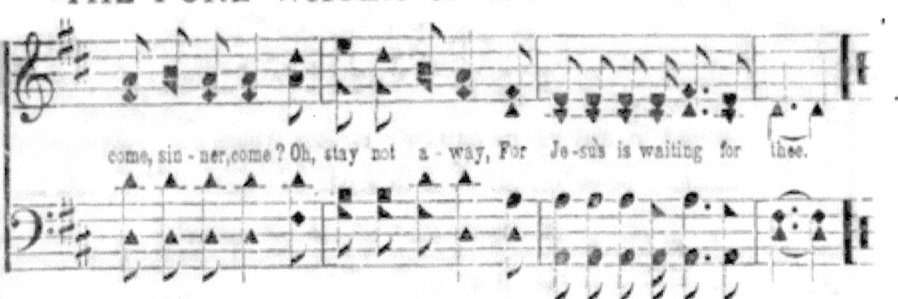

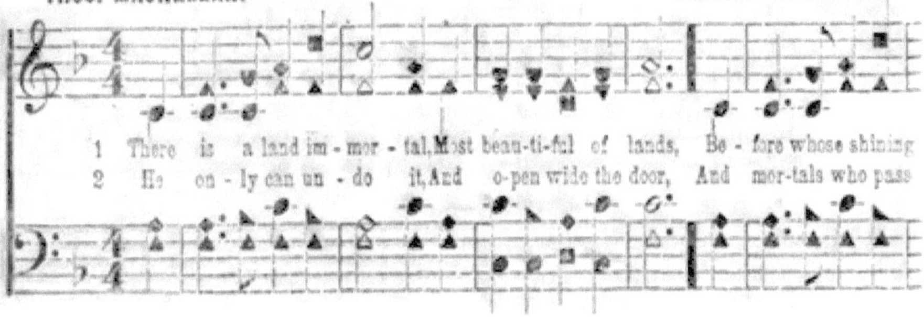

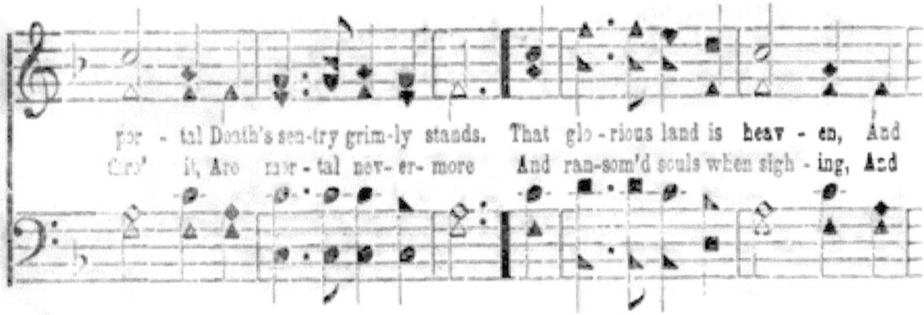

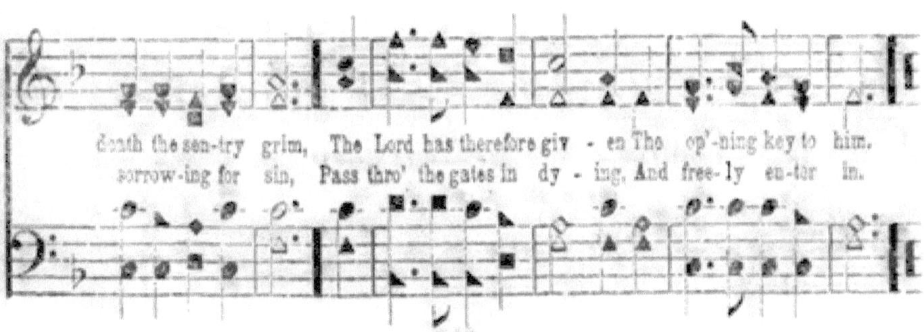

HAPPY HOME. CONCLUDED.

We shall dwell in bliss and glory,
We shall dwell in bliss and glory in that home,
In that home, ... hap-py home.
In that home, hap-py home, hap-py home.

VALERIA. C. M.

C. J. MILLER.

1 My God, my Father, bliss-ful name! Oh, may I call thee mine;
2 What-e'er thy sa-cred will or-dains, O give me strength to bear!
May I with sweet as-sur-ance claim, A por-tion so di-vine.
And let me know my Fa-ther reigns, And trust his ten-der care.

I AM WAITING FOR A MESSAGE.

LEANDER WISE.   J. B. FERGUSON, by per.

DUET.

1. I am wait-ing for a mes-sage from the land of the real;
2. Sad and lone-ly I have wan-dered thro' this dark vale of tears,
3. Oh, I have the bless'd as-sur-ance from the great King of kings,
4. Lo! the light is grow-ing bright-er, and the mists clear a-way,

I am wait-ing as the time draw-eth nigh;.. I am
On my jour-ney to the sweet land of rest;.. Still I'm
That the treas-ure I have gar-nered a-bove,.. Gives me
As the dawn-ing of the day draw-eth nigh,.. That shall

wait-ing, and I'm long-ing To re-ceive the prom-ised bless-ing
wait-ing, and I'm long-ing To re-ceive the prom-ised bless-ing
ti-tle to the bless-ing For the which I've long been wait-ing
ush-er in the morn-ing That will bring the prom-ised bless-ing

That a-waits me in the sweet by and by.
That a-waits me in the land of the blest.
That a-waits me in the E-den of love.
That a-waits me in the sweet by and by.

CHORUS.

I am wait - - - ing, I am wait - - ing as the
I am wait-ing,   I am wait-ing,

time draw-eth nigh, To re-ceive the prom-ised bless-ing in the

BRING THE CHILDREN, ETC. CONCLUDED.

WHAT A GATH'RING, ETC. Concluded.

THE HALF HAS NOT BEEN TOLD.

ELIZA SHERMAN. FRANK M. DAVIS, by per.

AUTUMN LEAVES. Concluded.

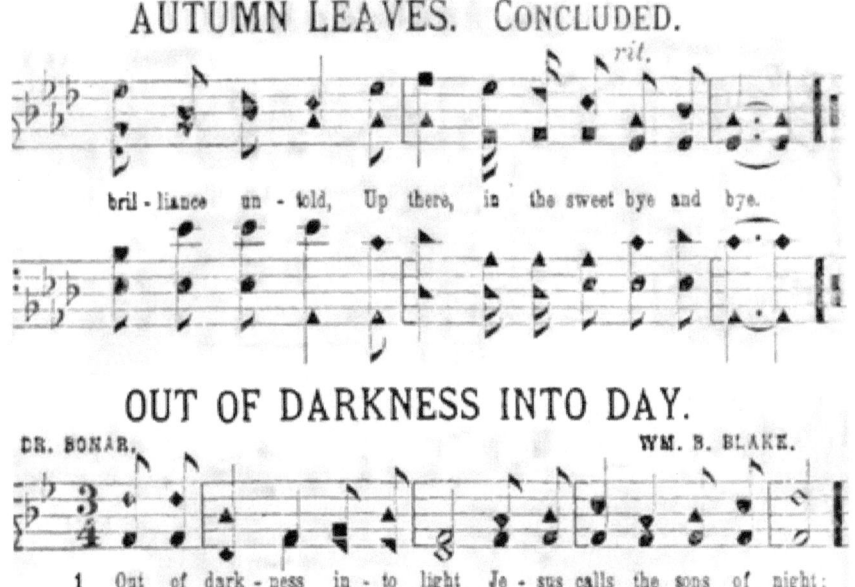

OUT OF DARKNESS INTO DAY.

DR. BONAR. WM. B. BLAKE.

1. Out of dark-ness in-to light Je-sus calls the sons of night;
2. From this world's al-lur-ing snares, From its per-ils and its cares,
3. From the van-i-ties of youth, In-to rest, and love, and truth,

Out of dark-ness in-to day Je-sus bids us come a-way.
From its van-i-ty and strife Je-sus beck-ons us to life.
In-to joy that nev-er palls, Je-sus in his mer-cy calls.

D.S. Out of dark-ness in-to day, Endless, ev-er-last-ing day.

CHORUS.

Come, oh, come, I am the light, I will chase a-way your night.

4

Into green pastures fair,
  I fain this day would go,
Beside the living stream
  Where healing waters flow
Thus till I reach the gate,
  And join the heavenly band,
Thus till my soul is saved
  Lord, take my hand.

I KNOW THAT JESUS SAVES ME.

Y. J. B. ATCHINSON.   A. J. SHOWALTER.

IN THE SHADOW OF THE ROCK. Concluded.

HEAR ME, SAVIOUR.

A. S. K.   ALDINE S. KIEFFER.

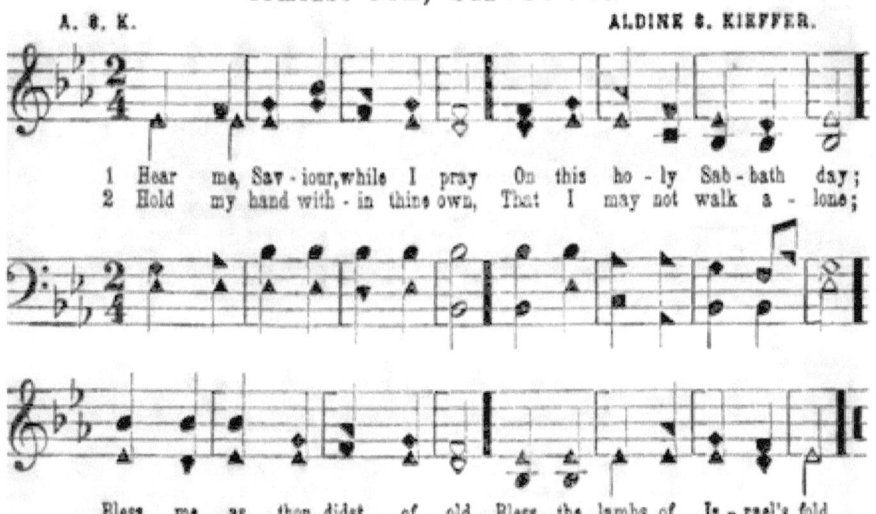

1. Hear me, Saviour, while I pray On this holy Sabbath day;
Bless me as thou didst of old Bless the lambs of Israel's fold.

2. Hold my hand within thine own, That I may not walk alone;
Guide my foot-steps lest they stray Into sin's dark desert way.

3
Bless mine eyes that they may see
Light and life alone in thee;
Bless my heart that it may find
Joys of an immortal kind.

4
Bless my soul with Faith and Love,
Leading to thy courts above,—
There to praise thy name on high,
While eternal years go by.

LET US TELL THE SAME OLD STORY. Concl'd.

Let us tell the same old story, Of salvation full and free,
Tell of Jesus and his glory, Tell of Christ on Calvary;
Some may hear it by the wayside, Burdened by the weight of sin,
Now while mercy's door is open, They may all be gathered in.

THE MANSIONS OF LOVE. CONCLUDED.

ALL IN ALL. CONCLUDED.

3 And now my soul is heavenward bent,
   With speed of angel's wing 'tis sent;
   This heaven's border-land may be,
   Yet there's a fairer o'er the sea,—
   A fairer, for its glorious light
   Is never dimmed by cloud or night,
   And all our souls, blood-washed and free,
   The King in glorious beauty see.

4 The earth's redeemed and ransomed bands,
   Clasp golden harps in blood-washed hands;
   And from their lips, o'er valleys free,
   Float strains of richest melody:
   And, oh! I soon shall join that throng,
   And sing with them redemption's song,
   For this fair land and crown of life,
   I soon shall change life's tears and strife!

THE WINDS BREATHE LOW.

J. H. T., Feb., 24, 1882.

2 How beautiful on all the hills
   The crimson light is shed!
   'Tis like the peace the Christian gives
   To mourners round his bed.

3 How mildly on the wandering cloud
   The sunset beam is cast!
   'Tis like the memory left behind,
   When loved ones breathe their last.

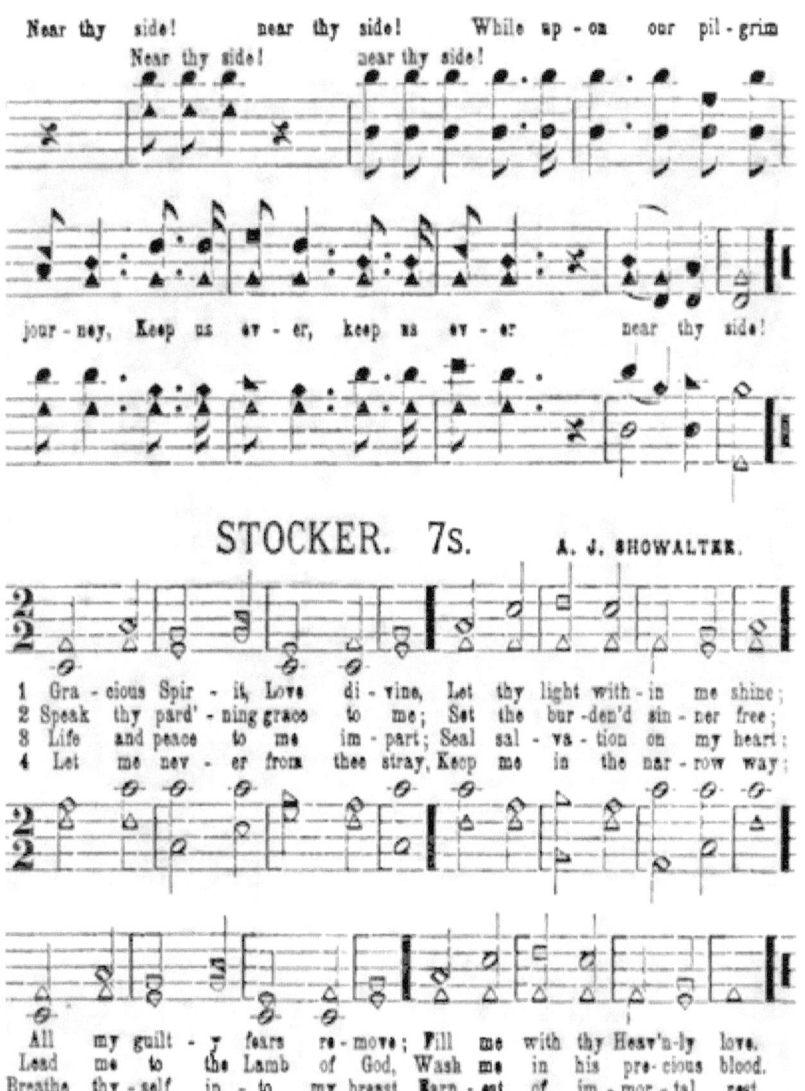

IN THE SWEET FIELDS OF EDEN. Concluded

4
Sing, O sing, ye heirs of glory;
　Shout your triumph as ye go;
Zion's gate will open for you,
　You shall find an entrance through;
Death itself shall then be vanquished,
　And his sting shall be withdrawn;
Shout for gladness, O ye ransomed,
　Hail with joy the rising morn.
　　Chorus.—In the sweet fields, etc.

2
Thou, O "Rock," like Zion's mountain,
  A strong shelter doth afford,
And the thirsty find a fountain
  Flowing from that Rock, the Lord.
Am I weary, heavy laden,
  In this present weary land?
Here's the Rock whose cooling shadows
  Lie across life's burning sand.

3
Thus I'm safe in danger's hour,
  Ever have a refuge nigh,
Simply trusting in the power
  Of the "Higher Rock" than I.
'Rock of Ages," I will ever,
  Ever, ever trust in Thee,
And my peace shall as a river
  Flow to all eternity.

I'LL BE THERE.
"FREEDMAN'S SONG."
Arr. by A. J. S.

2 His track I see and I'll pursue,
  When the last trumpet sounds, I'll be there,
The narrow way, till Him I view,
  When the last trumpet sounds, I'll be there.

3 This is the way I long have sought,
  When the last trumpet sounds, I'll be there,
And mourned because I found it not,
  When the last trumpet sounds, I'll be there.

ASK, SEEK, KNOCK. CONCLUDED.

k, seek, knock, A bless-ing is wait-ing for thee.

HAIL TO THE BRIGHTNESS. WM. B. BLAKE.

il to the bright-ness of Zi-on's day! And joy to the
il to the bright-ness of Zi-on's day! So long by the
e from all lands, from the is-land's shore, Praise to Je-ho-

that in dark-ness lay; Hail to the mil-lions from
-ets of God fore-told; Hush'd be the ac-cents of
as-cends to the sky! En-gines of war now are

D.S. Sing hal-le-lu-jah! the

-age set free, Hail to the morn of our glad ju-bi-lee.
row's deep lay, Zi-on, in tri-umph the Sav-iour be-hold!
to the dust, Shouts of sal-va-tion are rend-ing the sky.

draw-eth near! Soon we shall with Him in glo-ry ap-pear.

JESUS! THE VERY THOUGHT IS SWEET.

A. J. SHOWALTER.

1. Jesus!— the ver-y thought is sweet, In that dear Name all heart-joys meet; But sweet-er than sweet hon-ey far The glimps-es of His pres-ence are.
2. No word is sung more sweet than this; No name is heard more full of bliss; No thought brings sweet-er com-fort nigh, Than Je-sus, Son of God most high. A-men.

3. Jesus, Thou sweetness, pure and blest,
   Truth's Fountain, Light of souls distressed,
   Surpassing all that heart requires,
   Exceeding all that soul desires!

4. I seek for Jesus in repose,
   When round my heart its chambers close;
   Abroad, and when I shut the door,
   I long for Jesus evermore. AMEN.

OVER THERE. CONCLUDED.

HARTWELL.

A. S. K.

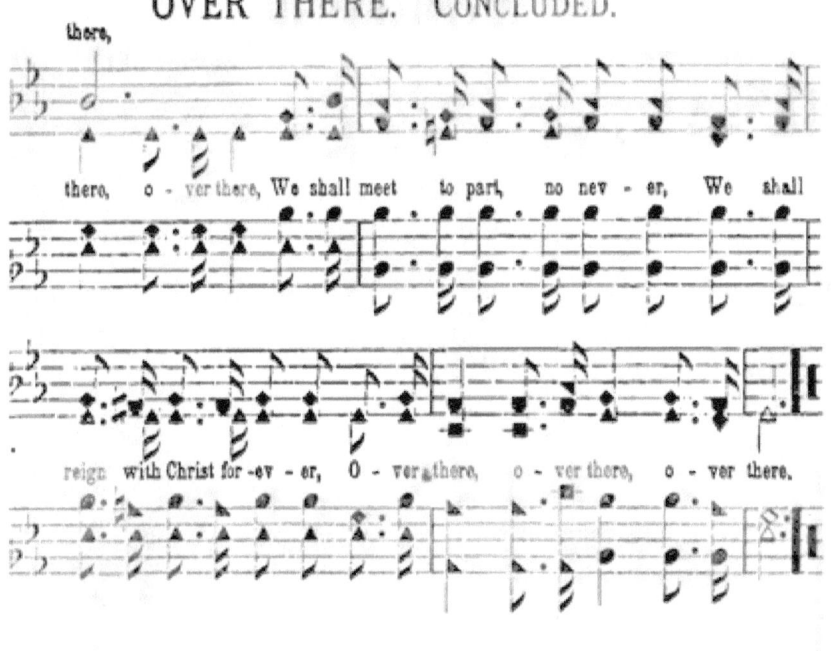

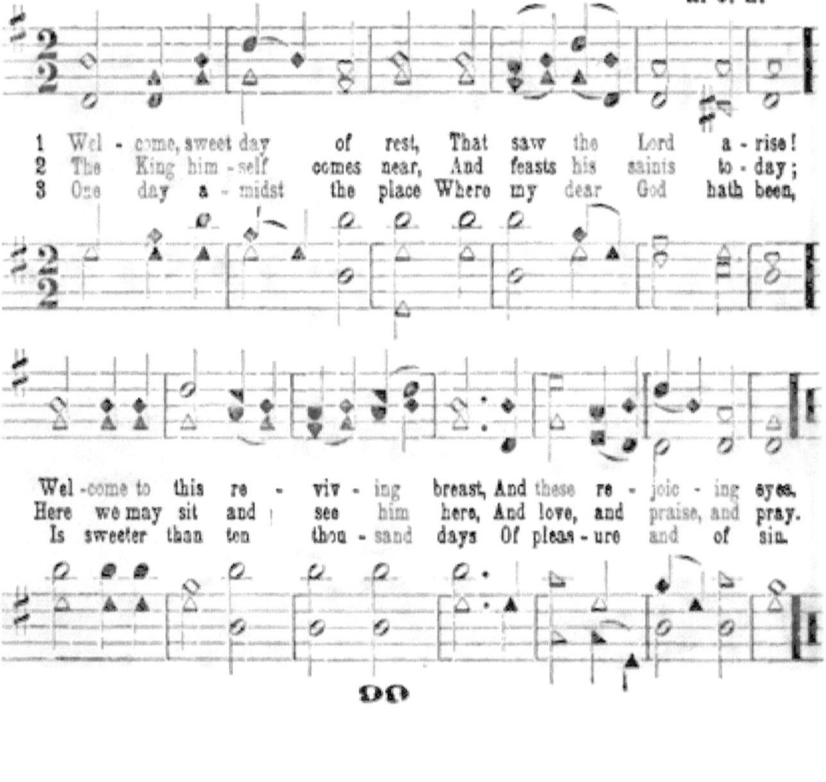

JOYFULLY SING. Concluded.

joy-ful-ly sing, To Him who reigns, our
An-chor and our Hope, Joy-ful-ly sing, joy-ful-ly sing.

HAPPY HOME. C. M.

1 Hap-py the home when God is there, And love fills ev'-ry breast;
2 Hap-py the home where Je-sus' name Is sweet to ev'-ry ear;
When one their wish, and one their prayer, And one their heav'nly rest.
Where chil-dren ear-ly lisp his fame, And par-ents hold him dear.

HAPPY NEWS. Concluded.

Hap-py news,
Happy news, hap-py news,
Hap-py news, happy news for-ev-er-more.

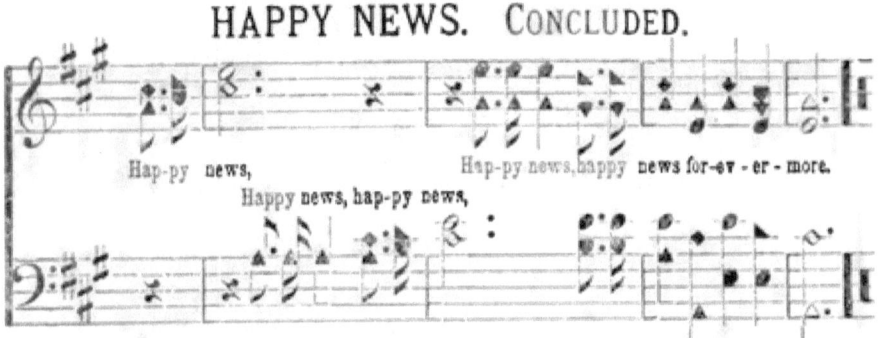

3 Happy news let all be telling,
Tidings glad we carol, too;
May the mighty chorus swelling
Pierce the darken'd ages through.

4 Lord of Lords, and King of glory!
How we love His praise to sing;
Youth so tender, age so hoary,
All may call the Saviour King.

ERNEST. S. M.

J. W. K. J. W. Kounse.

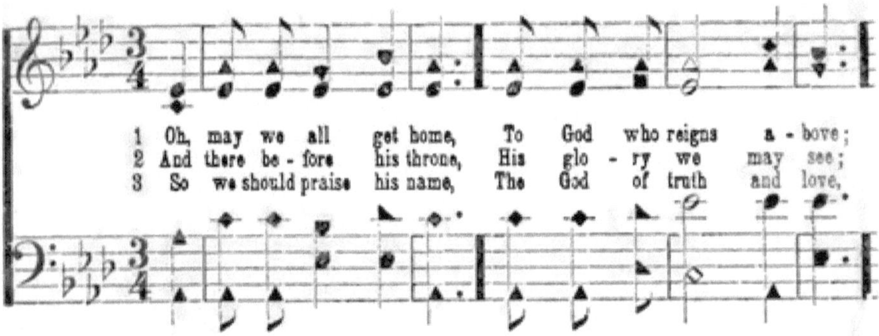
1 Oh, may we all get home, To God who reigns a-bove;
2 And there be-fore his throne, His glo-ry we may see;
3 So we should praise his name, The God of truth and love,

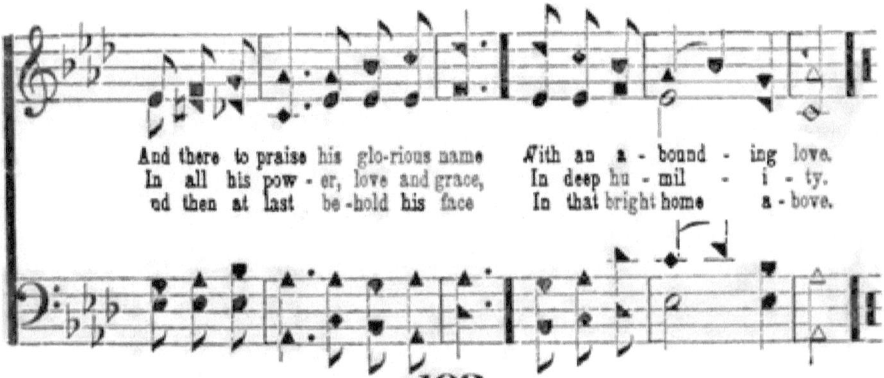
And there to praise his glo-rious name With an a-bound-ing love.
In all his pow-er, love and grace, In deep hu-mil-i-ty.
nd then at last be-hold his face In that bright home a-bove.

MY FEET, MY HANDS.

REV. C. W. RAY. CHAS. EDW. PRIOR, by per.

1 Jesus, guide my little feet A-long the heav'n-ly way;
  Safely guard them from each snare, Lest they should go a-stray;
  I shall be sure to turn a-side, Un-less my foot-steps Thou shalt guide.

2 Jesus, help my little hands To do Thy ho-ly will;
  Ev'ry page in my life's book, Help me with good to fill.
  How sad life's re-cord, should I make No sac-ri-fice for Thy dear sake!

3
Jesus, touch my little eyes
  That I may always see
Work that waits my willing hands,
  And shows my love for Thee;
Help me to hear and heed Thy voice,
  And daily make Thy ways my choice.

4
Jesus, teach my little lips
  To tell thy wondrous love;
Change my prayers to songs of
  And bring me safe above.
In mansions bright prepared
Thy face and glory I shall

Copyright, 1882, by CHAS. EDW. PRIOR.

THOU SHALT REST AT EVE. CONCLUDED.

3

Though the promise long may tarry,
  And the way seem dark and drear,
Gloomy doubts and fears still parry,
  Night will soon be here:
Loved ones wait beyond the river,
  They no longer sin or grieve,
With them, in the bright forever,
  Thou shalt rest at eve.

UP AND DOING. CONCLUDED.

NEARER, YET NEARER.

A. S. KIEFFER.

2
Purer, yet purer, I long to be,
Surer, yet surer, My God, of Thee;
Still hoping, praying, Ever to be
Nearer, still nearer, My God, to Thee.

3
Higher, yet higher, Out of the night,
Nearer, yet nearer The throne of white,
Still rising higher, Nearer the light,
Nearer, still nearer The throne of white.

SPREAD THE GLAD EVANGEL. Concluded.

117

LET NOT THY HOPES DEPART. CONCLUDED.

VAUGHAN. 8s & 4s.

[For Male voices.]

J. H. T.

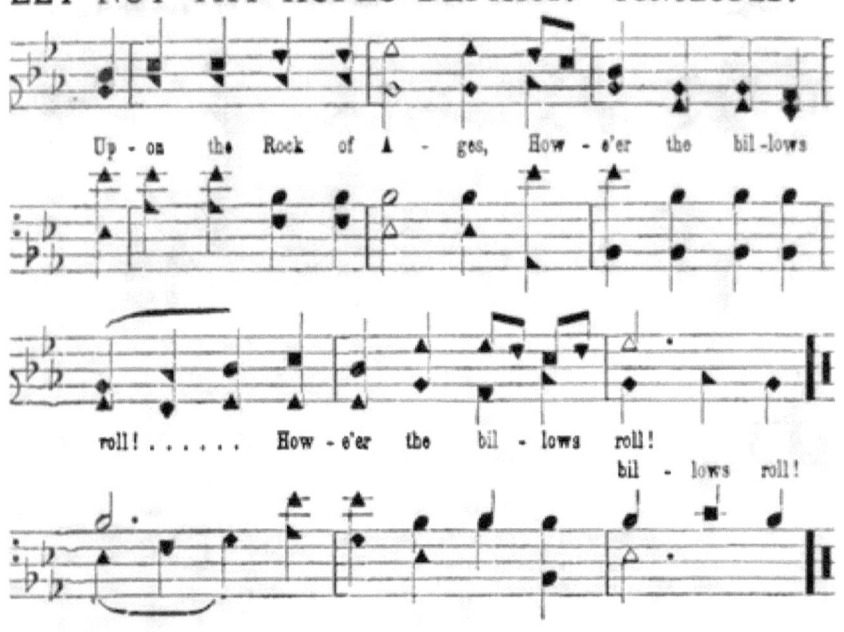

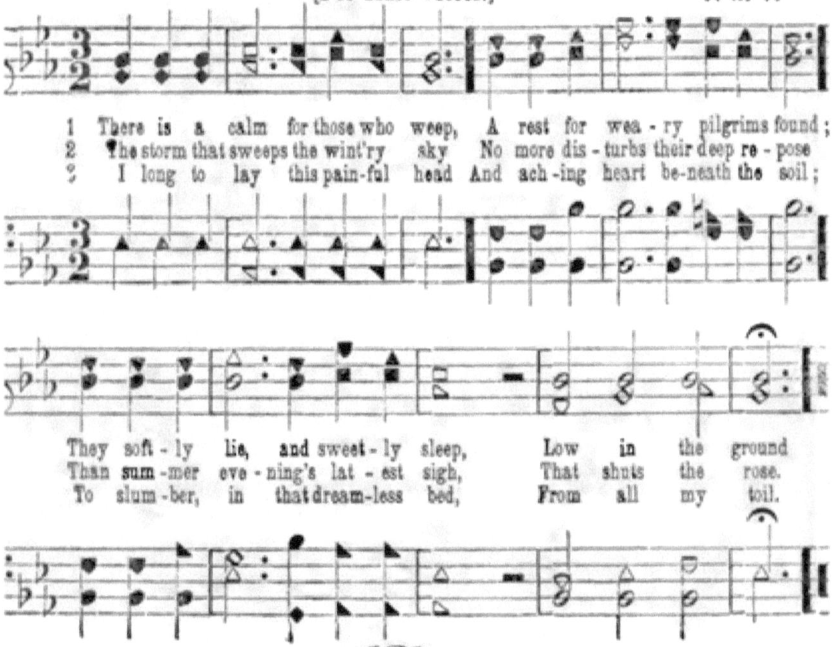

DRAWING NEARER.

F. M. D.
FRANK M. DAVIS.

1 Draw-ing near-er ev'-ry day, ev'-ry day, Near-er
2 Draw-ing near-er ev'-ry day, ev'-ry day, To the

to the soul's sweet home, soul's sweet home, Bright-er, bright-er grows the
land of rest a-bove, rest a-bove, Je-sus kind-ly leads the

way, grows the way, As we near the heav'n-ly dome.
way, leads the way, Through his sym-pa-thiz-ing love.

CHORUS.

Near-er, near-er to the soul's sweet home, Sings the pilgrim on his way, . . .

DRAWING NEARER. CONCLUDED.

3 Drawing nearer every **day**,
　Nearer to the golden **strand**;
Clouds and darkness **flee** away,
　And reveal sweet Beulah land.

MENTOR. C. M.
A. N. JOHNSON.

COME TO THE WATERS OF LIFE. CONCLUDED.

REFRAIN.

Come, come, come, Come to the wa-ters of life.

Come, come, come, Come to the wa-ters of life.

SAVIOUR, COMFORT ME.   A. S. K.

1 In the dark and drear-y day, When earth's rich-es flee a-way,
2 When the i-dols all are gone, That my poor heart yearned up-on,
3 Thou who wast so sore-ly tried, In the dark-ness cru-ci-fied,
4 So it shall be good for me, Much af-flict-ed now to be,

And the last hope will not stay, Sav-iour, com-fort me, Sav-iour, com-fort me.
Des-o-late, be-reft, a-lone, Sav-iour, com-fort me, Sav-iour, com-fort me.
Bid me in thy love con-fide, Sav-iour, com-fort me, Sav-iour, com-fort me.
If thou wilt but ten-der-ly, Sav-iour, com-fort me, Sav-iour, com-fort me.

INDEX.

Airhart,	27
All in All,	74
Army of the Lord,	36
Ask, Seek, Knock,	92
Autumn Leaves,	60
Blessed Jubilee,	67
Bless the Lord,	10
Bringing in the Sheaves,	6
Bring the Children to the Saviour,	46
Callie,	19
Canaan-Land,	52
Come, Gracious Spirit,	57
Come to the Cross of Jesus,	16
Come to the Waters of Life,	124
Come, ye Disconsolate,	37
Come ye that Love the Lord,	34
Cross of Christ,	106
Drawing Nearer,	122
Endo,	34
Ernest.—S. M.,	103
Evening Bells,	66
Evening Hymn,	31
Faith, Hope, and Love,	5
Gates of the Beautiful,	43
Georgiana,	85
God's Care,	83
Greeneville,	13
Hail to the Brightness,	93
Happy Home,	38
Happy Home.—C. M.	101
Happy News,	102
Hartwell,	99
Hear me, Saviour,	65
Hear my Cry,	41
His Kind words Can never Die,	58
Homeward Bound,	11
I am Coming to the Cross,	82
I am Waiting,	12
I am Waiting for a Message,	44
I Know that Jesus Saves me,	63
I'll be There,	89
In Climes Above,	90

In the Blood of the Lamb,	118
In the Harbor,	35
In the Hour of Trial,	84
In the Shadow of his Wing,	24
In the Shadow of the Rock,	64
In the Sweet Fields of Eden,	78
I Shall be Satisfied,	56
Is my Name Written There,	55
Jefferson,	45
Jehovah Jireh,	3
Jesus, the Very Thought is Sweet,	96
Joyfully Sing,	100
Kneeling at the Threshold,	14
Land Immortal,	29
Leave Me Not,	21
Leaving The Rest With Jesus,	53
Let Not Thy Hopes Depart,	120
Let us Tell the same Old Story,	68
Lord, Take My Hand,	62
Lulemon,	25
Marching to Zion,	30
Markell,	15
Mentor.—C. M.,	123
My Feet, My Hands,	107
Nearer, Yet Nearer,	115
Near Thy Side,	76
Olden Memories,	32
One Day Nearer Home,	26
On to Victory,	18
Out of Darkness Into Day,	61
Over Jordan,	88
Over There,	98
Palm Bearers,	72
Parting,	111
Pleasant are Thy Courts Above,	73
Pray for the Wanderer,	8
Remember.—C. M.,	105
Rest In Me,	49
Rest, Weary One,	23
Ring the Bells,	94
Rock of Ages (New),	81
Roll on, Dark Stream,	4
Safe at Home,	86
Saviour, Comfort Me,	125

Schiller,	7
Shall We Meet Thee,	42
Showers of Blessing,	20
Song of Praise,	59
Spread the Glad Evangel,	116
Stocker,	77
Sweet Land of Rest,	9
Sweetly We'll Sing,	40
Tell Us Something More,	22
The Half Has Not Been Told,	54
The Happy Place,	87
The Mansions of Love,	70
The Nearer I Keep to Jesus,	48
The Pure Water of Life,	28
The Shepherd is calling,	80
The Sycamore Bough,	97
The Winds Breathe Low,	57
They Shall Shine as the Stars,	112
Those Christmas Bells,	33
Thou shalt Rest at Eve,	108
Trusting All to Jesus,	110
Trusting in Jesus,	17
Up and Doing,	114
Urvilla.—L. M.	119
Valeria,	31
Vaughan,	121
Waiting,	91
Wakefield,	113
What a Gathering that will be,	50
Willing Workers,	104
Zion's King, 7s,	95

Music Typography by
J. M. ARMSTRONG & CO.,
710 Sansom Street,
Philadelphia, Penna.

www.ingramcontent.com/pod-product-compliance
Lightning Source LLC
Chambersburg PA
CBHW020109170426
43199CB00009B/460